*Here are some other nonfiction
Redfeather Books you will enjoy*

Alligators: A Success Story
by Patricia Lauber

Caves! Underground Worlds
by Jeanne Bendick

*Earthworms: Underground Farmers
by Patricia Lauber

*Exploring an Ocean Tide Pool
by Jeanne Bendick

*Frozen Man
by David Getz

*Great Whales: The Gentle Giants
by Patricia Lauber

Life on Mars
by David Getz

Lighthouses: Watchers at Sea
by Brenda Z. Guiberson

*Salmon Story
by Brenda Z. Guiberson

*Available in paperback

IN SEARCH OF THE
GRAND CANYON

IN SEARCH OF THE
GRAND CANYON

With illustrations by the author
MARY ANN FRASER

A REDFEATHER BOOK
Henry Holt and Company · *New York*

Unless otherwise noted, the black-and-white photos were taken during Powell's second expedition down the Colorado River in 1871–72. There was no photographer present on the 1869 expedition. The etchings in this book were produced by artists hired to illustrate Powell's later reports. Much of their work was based on photographs.

I wish to acknowledge the Green River Chamber of Commerce, Susan Whetstone of the Utah State Historical Society, Betty White of the Canyonlands National Park Division of Interpretation, and Greer Price with the Division of Interpretation at Grand Canyon National Park for their assistance.

Henry Holt and Company, Inc.
Publishers since 1866
115 West 18th Street
New York, New York 10011

Henry Holt is a registered trademark of Henry Holt and Company, Inc.

Library of Congress Cataloging-in-Publication Data
Fraser, Mary Ann. In search of the Grand Canyon: down the Colorado with John
Wesley Powell / by Mary Ann Fraser.
p.   cm.—(A Redfeather Book). Includes bibliographical references.
1. Colorado River (Colo.-Mexico—Discovery and exploration—Juvenile literature.
2. Grand Canyon (Ariz.)—Discovery and exploration—Juvenile literature. 3. Powell,
John Wesley, 1834–1902—Journeys—Colorado River (Colo.-Mexico)—Juvenile
literature. [1. Colorado River (Colo.-Mexico)—Discovery and exploration. 2. Grand
Canyon (Ariz.)—Discovery and exploration. 3. Powell, John Wesley, 1834–1902.] I.
Title. II. Series: Redfeather books.
F788.F76 1995 979.1'—dc20 94-38087

ISBN 0-8050-3495-1 (hardcover)
3 5 7 9 10 8 6 4 2

ISBN 0-8050-5543-6 (paperback)
1 3 5 7 9 10 8 6 4 2

First published in hardcover in 1995 by Henry Holt and Company, Inc.
First Redfeather paperback edition, 1997

Printed in Mexico

For Peri

CONTENTS

IN SEARCH OF THE
GRAND CANYON

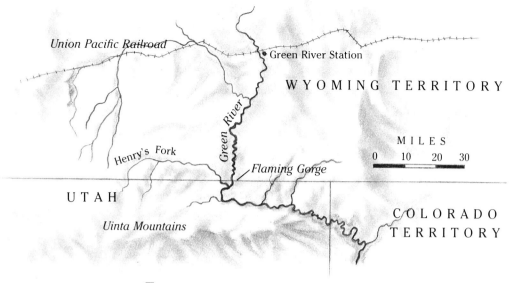

Union Pacific Railroad

● Green River Station

W Y O M I N G T E R R I T O R Y

Green River

Henry's Fork

M I L E S
0   10   20   30

Flaming Gorge

U T A H

Uinta Mountains

C O L O R A D O
T E R R I T O R Y

1 TESTING THE WATERS

On May 24, 1869, Major John Wesley Powell and his nine-man crew launched their boats at Green River Station, Wyoming Territory. They were about to challenge the uncharted canyons of the Colorado River and its main tributary, the Green.

Today the Colorado River is the most fought-over water system in the world. Its waters are used to grow grapes in New Mexico, float rafts in Arizona, brew beer in Colorado, fill swimming pools in California, water golf courses in Nevada, and nourish cantaloupes in Mexico. But in 1869 most people thought the Colorado River system was a "profitless locality."

The major was one of the first to appreciate the Colorado River region and to understand what it could mean to the country. A self-taught scientist, he had dreamed for many years of exploring and charting the river and its many canyons, especially its largest and most spectacular, the Grand Canyon.

Though he had lost his right arm below the elbow in a bloody Civil War battle, he was determined to run the river. He knew how important this area would be to the future of the nation.

With the ending of the Civil War and the completion of the transcontinental railroad, Americans were moving out in all directions. New settlers were discovering what the land had to offer and claiming it for their own, even if American Indians already occupied it. Powell's expedition came in the midst of these changes and conflicts.

A talented organizer, Major Powell had spent

The Colorado River has the greatest elevational drop of all the waterways in North America. It is also one of the siltiest and saltiest, carrying almost four million tons of material a day.

three years gathering survey documents from Mormon missionaries and the U.S. government, and speaking with Indians, settlers, and trappers along the Green River. But there was much he did not know. No one had ever successfully navigated the upper Colorado River or the Grand Canyon, and maps showed the region as a five-hundred-mile-long blank.

Although Native American cultures had inhabited the Colorado River basin for thousands of years, the recorded history of the Grand Canyon did not begin until 1540, when conquistadores first peered over its rim. During the next three hundred years rugged mountain men, early explorers, prospectors bound for California gold, and frontiersmen guiding settlers had crossed the Green and Colorado Rivers many times. Most had viewed the canyons as mere obstacles to reaching their final destinations.

That afternoon Powell's boats sat low in the muddy water, loaded down with scientific instruments and enough supplies for ten months. A thirty-seven-star American flag mounted on the lead boat waved in the breeze. Pushed by the swollen Green River, the boats soon left the train bridge far behind and the town faded out of sight.

For the first sixty miles through Wyoming badlands, the ten-man expedition's main problems were learning to work together and how to steer.

Powell's scientific knowledge and talents as a leader quickly won the respect of his volunteers. Unlike the major they had little river experience or scientific training. Most had joined the expedition hoping to find gold and adventure. But what the men lacked in experience and knowledge, they made up for in hardiness and a desire for action.

Jack Sumner, who had run a Denver trading post; Oramel Howland, a printer; Billy Hawkins, a Union Army veteran; and Bill Dunn, a former trapper and mule skinner, had served as Powell's guides and assistants during his explorations in the region the year before. Other members of the

The start at Green River

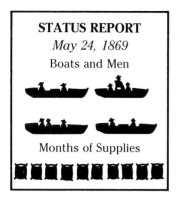
party included Captain Walter Powell, the major's brother, who had been imprisoned during the Civil War; Seneca Howland, also a Civil War veteran and Oramel Howland's brother; and George Bradley, who enlisted after Powell arranged to have him discharged from the army. At the last moment, well-to-do Englishman Frank Goodman, and eighteen-year-old drifter Andrew Hall joined the party at Green River Station.

The Green River, which begins in the highlands of the Wind River Mountains, bore Powell's specially designed boats along with tons of churning sand, mud, and gravel. Struggling with the stocky oars, the men wound their way down the river between bluffs of shale and limestone.

Usually the boats traveled in order. Major Pow-

Specially designed by Powell, each boat had two watertight compartments to store supplies and keep afloat. *Emma Dean* was sixteen feet long and made of lightweight pine for fast rowing. *Kitty Clyde's Sister*, *No Name*, and *Maid of the Canyon* were twenty-one feet long, made of oak, and could each carry two and a quarter tons of cargo.

Rudder Oar

ell and his boatmen led the way in the *Emma Dean*, which was named after Powell's wife. The major sat in a chair strapped to the boat. From there he could send information about the river with flag signals to the men behind. Following the pilot boat were *Kitty Clyde's Sister*, *No Name*, and finally *Maid of the Canyon*.

On May 27, at the foot of the Uinta Mountains, the ten voyagers arrived at their first canyon. The canyon's twelve hundred foot walls were formed of brilliant red and orange rock, and looked as if they were on fire. The men dubbed it "Flaming Gorge."

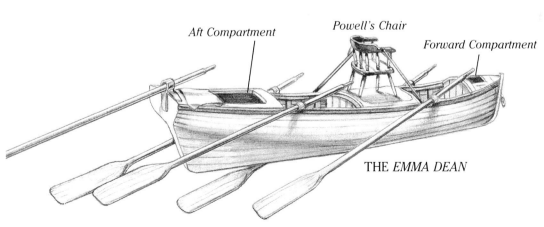

Aft Compartment   Powell's Chair   Forward Compartment

THE *EMMA DEAN*

This is Flaming Gorge today. It was dramatically changed in 1963 with the completion of Flaming Gorge Dam. Photo by Gary Ladd

Amidst the canyon's colored bands Powell found the fossils of ancient marine animals. These sea creatures had lived in the oceans that had once covered the western part of the continent.

Over millions of years advancing and retreating oceans and rivers had left thick deposits of sand and limestone. The pressure of overlying layers and filtering water had cemented these sediments into solid rock. Forces in the earth then lifted these layers, forming the Colorado Plateau, or, as Powell called it, the "Plateau Province."

After collecting the fossils, the men made an easy run through Flaming Gorge. But when they came to their first set of rapids, they grew nervous. The previous spring, an old Paiute Indian named Pa'-ri-ats had told Powell about a family

The Theory of Antecedent Rivers

This theory was perhaps Powell's greatest contribution to geology. He believed that the Green River was older than the mountains. The river continued to downcut and maintain its original course as the mountains uplifted by faulting and folding.

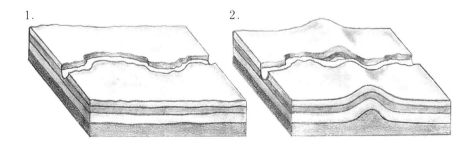

1.   2.

from his tribe who drowned trying to run this same canyon. Mountaineers who lived in the region had also warned that the river could not be navigated.

Powell stood on deck, guiding the oarsmen between jagged rocks and away from the overhanging ledges. Faster and faster the wooden vessels leaped over the rolling waves like deer over fallen timber. The roar of the rapids drowned the men's voices. Foaming crests broke over the boats and drenched the men with bone-chilling water.

After many stops to bail out the boats, the travelers reached calm water. They had successfully run their first rapids and felt both relieved and proud. But their joy did not last long. A short distance downriver they heard the thunderous roar of a waterfall.

Powell realized that the falls were too risky—they would have to "line" the boats, which meant getting out and letting them down with ropes.

Once the boats were safely past the waterfall, the men portaged, or carried, the cargo down the steep and rocky trail beside the falls. There they discovered an inscription in red: "Ashley 1825." The words had been painted by General William Ashley, who was the leader of an earlier expedition. All members of the expedition had drowned

Lining the Boats

To line a boat the men tied a rope to the bow, or front, and another to the stern, or back. The bowline was taken to the bottom of the fall and secured. Then five or six men held the stern line and slowly lowered the boat downriver. When they could no longer hold the boat against the current, they let go, and the boat tumbled to the bottom of the fall where it was hauled in with the bowline.

in one of the later canyons except for Ashley and one other man.

For Powell and his companions, the inscription was a warning that dangerous waters lay ahead. In honor of the man who had gone before them, they named the cascade "Ashley Falls."

2 MISHAPS AND DISASTERS

On the morning of June 6, 1869, the chorus of songbirds was interrupted by the cook Hawkins's call to breakfast. "Roll out! Roll out! Bulls in the corral! Chain up the gaps! Roll out!" Hawkins had been an ox driver on a wagon train. But covered wagons had little future now that railroad trains ran from the Atlantic to the Pacific.

Only a month earlier, the first train to cross the North American continent had rumbled through Green River Station. Soon the transcontinental railroad would be bringing thousands of settlers to the west. Land speculators and promoters had described the dusty plains and deserts as lush and fertile. But most of the land that settlers claimed was actually dry and dusty. In order to survive, they would need water from the Colorado River and its tributaries. Powell suspected there was enough water to supply only a fraction of the territory. His expedition was the first real effort to chart this vital river system and note areas where irrigation would be possible.

The ten men broke camp, reloaded the boats, and began another day on the river. In the late afternoon they arrived at the head of a canyon. Unsure of what lay ahead, they camped at its gaping mouth.

The next morning two or three of the men, including Powell, scaled the cliffs. Powell later admitted in his diary that it had taken many years of climbing to overcome his fear of heights. Now he could sit calmly on the edge of a cliff, his feet dangling into space. Perched two thousand feet

Powell's Scientific Instruments

Powell recorded the measurements, and Oramel Howland used them to make a map of the canyon and its features.

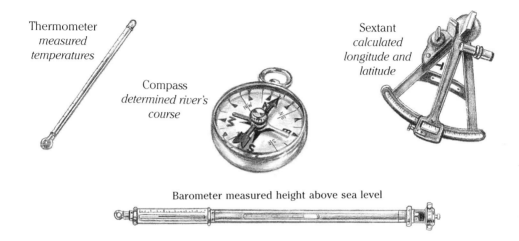

Thermometer *measured temperatures*

Compass *determined river's course*

Sextant *calculated longitude and latitude*

Barometer measured height above sea level

above the river, he wrote a letter to the *Chicago Tribune*, dated June 7, 1869.

Now, as I write, the sun is going down, and the shadows are settling in the canyon. The vermillion gleams and the rosy hues, the green and grey tints, are changing to sombre brown above, and the black shadows below. Now 'tis a black portal to a region of gloom.

And that is the gateway through which we enter our voyage of exploration tomorrow—and what shall we find?

They found rapids. Large boulders, which had sheered off cliffs or washed down from side canyons, caused churning spillovers. Treacherous side currents spun the boats broadside.

As the men battled the river, the sun burned the back of their necks and ears. Sand and silt washed up under their clothes, scratching and rubbing their skin raw. The constant dunkings and spray kept them soaked.

That night at supper the exhausted travelers huddled around a driftwood fire. As they talked about the day's furious rapids, Andy Hall remembered Robert Southey's poem "The Cataract of Lodore." The poem tells how "The Cataract strong/ Then plunges along,/ Striking and raging/

Lodore Canyon looking down through the Gates of Lodore
Photograph Archives, Utah State Historical Society

As if a war waging." Today the gorge is named the "Canyon of Lodore."

The next afternoon Powell again heard the tell-tale booming of a waterfall. The *Emma Dean* landed, and Powell left his oarsmen behind to signal the others while he hiked downstream to take a look.

Frank Goodman and Oramel and Seneca Howland were busy bailing out their boat and missed the signal. Like an arrow, they shot over the falls. Powell helplessly watched the *No Name* tumble down the twelve foot drop and then smash into a boulder. The shock sent the oars flying overboard. Out of control, the boat slammed into another rock. It snapped in two and its passengers were flung into the frothy river.

The Howland brothers washed up on a small sandbar. Fifty feet away in a whirlpool, Frank Goodman clung to a rock for dear life. If he didn't get help soon, he would drown. Working together, the brothers wrenched a root from the drift on the bar. They reached out to Frank and pulled him to safety.

But the danger was not over. The sandbar, which was just above another waterfall and surrounded by swift currents, was slowly disappearing in the rising river.

Finally Sumner arrived in the *Emma Dean* and managed to rescue his stranded companions. When the four men safely returned to the riverbank, the other members of the expedition rushed to greet them, Powell wrote, "as if they had been on a voyage around the world and wrecked on a distant coast."

Though the men were safe, the *No Name* was destroyed, and two thousand pounds of supplies were lost to the river. With one third of

their food gone, the expedition would have to move faster. The *No Name*'s crew could borrow clothes and bedding, and parts of the maps could be redrawn from memory. But without the barometers to measure elevation, Powell could not determine their progress down the river or chart the canyons.

He peered at the section of the *No Name* that was lodged on a boulder in the middle of the river. Could the barometers still be in its cabin?

To his surprise the next morning, Powell found the boat snagged on a rock only fifty feet downriver. Sumner and Dunn managed to navigate the currents to the wreck and returned with treasure—a package of thermometers, candles for reading instruments at night, a keg of whiskey, and the barometers.

After portaging and lining past a mile of hair-raising rapids, they discovered an oven lid, some tin plates, and a few other items on a sandy beach. Powell felt sure these were from Ashley's wreck and named the river stretch "Disaster Falls."

The next several days were, as Powell later wrote, "still rocks, rapids and portages." Everything was wet. The flour and coffee were soggy and gritty. Even the beans were sprouting. There

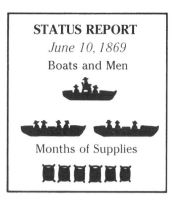

STATUS REPORT
June 10, 1869
Boats and Men

Months of Supplies

were no game animals within the canyon walls, and the few fish the men caught were bony and tasteless.

The major's military style was also beginning to irritate the men. Bradley complained in his journal about Powell's choice of campsites and that he felt like a galley slave.

Late in the afternoon of the sixteenth, the men made their camp among the trees that lined the bank. Then Powell set off alone to explore.

Suddenly a whirlwind sent sparks from the campfire into the dead willows and cedar sprays. Before the men could react, they were surrounded by a blazing fire. The racing flames scorched their clothes, singed their hair, and burned Bradley's ears as they darted for the moored boats. In the blinding heat and smoke, Hawkins grabbed the mess kit, jumped for the boat and fell into ten feet of water. The cooking equipment tumbled into the river. With no time to search for it, the men cut the boats free and headed into the unknown currents ahead.

Downriver they found Powell, and together they returned to the burned-out camp. Only a few pieces of clothing and bedding, some tin cups, basins, three spoons, and a kettle could be sal-

Fire in camp

vaged. From that point on, the men had to either share utensils or eat with their hands.

The next day, June 17, the expedition emerged out of the Canyon of Lodore and arrived at the mouth of the Yampa River. For the first time in ten days the constant roar of rapids did not fill their ears. At last there was quiet.

The journey through the canyon had been a never-ending story of miseries and disasters. But the men would always remember the many scenic wonders within those towering walls: the cliffs and crags, the amphitheaters and alcoves, the pinnacles and peaks, all in a rainbow of colors.

The men rested and caught up on their journals, charting, mapping, and letter writing. Oramel Howland wrote to the *Rocky Mountain News*:

> Our trip thus far has been pretty
> severe: still very exciting. When we
> have to run rapids, nothing is more
> exhilarating . . . and as a breaker
> dashes over us we shoot out from one

side or the other, after having run
the fall, one feels like hurrahing. A
calm, smooth stream, running only
at the rate of five or six miles per hour,
is a horror we all detest now.

Not all of the thrills and danger were on the river. On June 18, the expedition's leader nearly fell off a cliff. Bradley and Powell had climbed six hundred feet up to survey the route when Powell suddenly realized he could not let go to move up or down. Bradley saved him by removing his trousers and using them to pull the major to safety.

Over the next several days the party rowed through a narrow gorge Powell called "Whirlpool Canyon." At first the oarsmen fought to keep the boats straight. But when the men realized there was little danger in running with the twisting currents, they let the boats waltz along.

Finally the canyons opened up, and the expedition arrived at the mouth of the Uinta River.

Slowed by portaging, lining, and reloading, the expedition had only traveled a short distance into Utah by June 28. Although Powell and his comrades had overcome many obstacles, they feared the worst was yet to come.

3 INDIANS OF THE CANYONS

Four days later, Major Powell, Frank Goodman, and Bill Hawkins hiked forty miles up the Uinta River valley toward the Uinta Indian reservation. There they hoped to replace the lost mess kit and send letters to friends and family.

Throughout the nineteenth century, the American government had made separate treaties with various American Indian nations. The treaties said that the government would pay for Indian lands with money and supplies, and that the Indians could "reserve" certain territories for themselves. These territories would stay free of taxes and other claims.

Many white settlers moving into the West did not respect these treaties. They demanded safe access to Indian lands. The federal government decided on a new policy. Indian nations were no longer considered independent powers, and any Indian who refused to be confined to a reservation was considered hostile.

Indians were moved onto land the settlers and miners didn't want. Dishonest reservation agents overcharged for cheap and inferior supplies and pocketed the extra cash. Poor living conditions and disease caused thousands of deaths. By the 1870s the reservations were a national scandal.

Powell respected the American Indians perhaps more then any other western explorer. He knew they had been treated unfairly and sympathized with their poor living conditions. While the U.S. Army waged war against the Indian nations, he traveled without a military escort or even a gun to study their languages and cultures. He hoped someday to use this knowledge to aid them in their search for a better future.

The morning after his arrival at the reservation, Powell went to see the Ute chief, Tsau-wi-at, and his wife. Proudly the Indians showed Powell their farms, which were located in an area with many streams. The Indians used the water to irrigate their fields of potatoes, wheat, turnips, melons, pumpkins, and other vegetables. The chief's wife explained how she wanted the Utes to learn the settlers' farming methods so they could improve their living conditions.

When, at last, it came time to leave, Frank Goodman announced that he would not be continuing on; he had seen enough adventure. The rest of Powell's men, however, were anxious to be off. The peaceful valley bored them, and they longed for the thrill of rapids.

On July 6, the now nine-man expedition left the mouth of the Uinta River and entered territories that were completely uncharted and unmapped. The quiet river grew rougher and the head winds stronger as the three small boats entered a barren canyon. Clublike cedars and stunted bushes clung to the crags. Natural passages carved out of stone by wind and water led from one canyon chamber to another. The expedition chose the name "Canyon of Desolation."

Desolation Canyon where the Green River circles Sumner's Amphitheater
Photo by Gary Ladd

On July 12, after days of bad rapids, the major spotted a long, dangerous channel with rocks on the left and huge waves passing under an overhang on the right. Powell decided to run it.

The crew of the *Emma Dean* made it safely, but Walter Powell and George Bradley in *Kitty Clyde's Sister* were sucked into the towering waves on the right and headed straight for the overhang. Suddenly a large swell pitched Bradley over the side. But his foot caught in the seat and he was dragged facedown through the water. Close to drowning, he somehow grabbed hold of the gunwale and pulled his head above water for a breath.

Helplessly the major watched his younger brother and Bradley speed toward the projecting cliff. To everyone's amazement, Walter Powell pulled the boat to safety in just six powerful strokes, seized Bradley, and pulled him in.

Goodman, the Howlands, and the major had each come close to death. Now Bradley had joined them. Who would be next?

Beyond the Canyon of Desolation conditions grew worse. Facing rapid after rapid, the men were forced to keep lining the boats. Every day they grumbled about the backbreaking work, lousy food, heat, and mosquitoes. While the crew never doubted Powell's bravery, they began to question his cautiousness and the delays caused by his scientific studies. But with stubborn determination Powell kept control of the group.

On July 13, the adventurers broke out into open desert country. The broad plains were

Labyrinth Canyon at a point called Saddle of the Bowknot
Photograph Archives, Utah State Historical Society

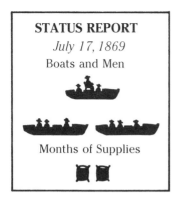

studded with buttes, hills, cliffs, and mountains that seemed to float in the reflected heat of midday.

Stroking with the oars, they made their way down the slow-moving Green River until they found an Indian crossing. This was one of the few places in all of the canyon wilderness where the river could be crossed. Here, in 1853, Captain John William Gunnison crossed the river while searching for a route for the Pacific Railroad.

Over the next several days, the winding river teased the weary travelers as it snaked through a maze they later named "Labyrinth Canyon." Eventually the towering cliffs spread open, and the men saw lofty buttes carved out of beautiful red sandstone. The Indians called it "Toom'-pin wu-near' Tu-weap'," or "Land of the Standing Rock."

The river dug into the rocks again, and the bluffs loomed higher and higher. Powell knew

Meeting of the Green and Colorado Rivers
Photo by National Park Service

from earlier reports that the joining of the Colorado and Green Rivers could not be far away. He stopped often to look for signs of the junction. Rumor had it that the meeting of the two rivers was marked by huge waterfalls and giant whirlpools. But Powell paid little attention to stories; he was only interested in facts.

Following the twisting river, they rowed, and watched, and waited.

In the late afternoon of July 17, they floated more than twelve hundred feet below the Colorado Plateau's surface. Then, with no other warning than the increased speed of the water, the mighty Colorado River joined the Green.

"Hurra! Hurra! Hurra!" wrote Bradley in his journal.

After almost two months and about 538 miles of difficult travel, they had lost only one boat and only one member had deserted the expedition. Powell's leadership and much criticized caution had fared them well. They were now a tight-knit expedition remaking the maps, and not the inexperienced band of trappers, ex-officers, printers, and adventurers who had started down the Green back in May.

Henry Mountains
Dirty Devil River
Cataract Canyon
Escalante River
Paria River
Colorado River
San Juan River
UTAH TERRITORY
Glen Canyon
Marble Canyon
ARIZONA TERRITORY
MILES
0 10 20 30 40
Little Colorado River

4 THE GRAND COLORADO RIVER

The Powell party spent the next three days exploring, taking measurements, and getting everything into shape for the journey ahead. They recaulked the damaged boats, sifted the lumpy flour, and repaired the battered barometers.

Their ten-month supply of food had dwindled to two months. Major Powell figured it would take at least that long to reach the end of their voyage.

On July 21, the expedition set off down the uncharted Colorado River. The cocoa-colored water ran deep and wide, but soon it broke into a series of churning rapids.

Major Powell did not want to chance losing any more of their provisions. The men lined and portaged whenever they could, and risked the rapids only when there was no other choice.

Above the men's heads, weathered pinnacles and crags crowned the towering walls. Below them, the water rolled and spilled violently. Huge, angular boulders filled the channel and broke the water into swirling whirlpools, wild chutes, and foaming breakers. Even Bradley, who would run any rapid Powell would let him, admitted some were too dangerous.

The men named the gorge "Cataract Canyon," and each day its fierce currents and jagged rocks pounded and scraped the boats.

While navigating through a narrow gorge on July 27, they spotted mountain sheep on the crags. After shooting a pair, the men feasted on fresh mutton and stale coffee. In his journal Bradley called it "the greatest event of the trip."

Past cataract after cataract the ragged crews carried their supplies. When the rapids were too dangerous for lining, they even carried the boats.

The canyon grew narrower until its walls met the river and nearly blocked the sunlight. There was no escape; the crew had to move with the swift current. The major stood in the *Emma Dean* while he searched for obstacles and listened for the roar of a fall. The twists and turns made it impossible for him to see what lay more than a few hundred feet ahead. After a mile and a half, the dark turned to light, and the weary travelers emerged from Cataract Canyon.

Floating on, they came to a smelly, mud-filled stream, which entered the Colorado from a side canyon. Dunn turned the *Emma Dean* into it so Powell could take a look.

Upon their return one of the men asked, "Is it a trout stream?"

"Naw, just a dirty-devil," cursed Dunn disgustedly. Oramel Howland marked the small, muddy river "Dirty Devil Creek" on the map. This was one of the last rivers to be named in North America.

From the mouth of the Dirty Devil, the Colorado River ran fast through a region of colorful rocks. Cliffs, buttes, and towering mountains lined the horizon. Now, instead of covering one to two miles a day, the travelers covered twenty.

Soon the party entered a canyon with low, red sandstone walls. Not far from its head they stumbled across the ancient ruins of a house two hundred feet above the river. The major believed the building had probably been three stories tall. He was fascinated with the arrowheads, pottery fragments, and flint chips that lay scattered at its base. Farther down the river, they found a group of ruins that included an L-shaped house with an underground ceremonial room or "kiva."

Powell suspected these ruins were built by early inhabitants of the canyons, whom he called the "Moqui." Today we use the word "Anasazi," which is a Navajo term meaning "Ancestors of our enemies."

The Anasazi were not the earliest inhabitants of the canyons. Hunter-gatherers of the Desert Culture lived in the region until about 1000 B.C. Their small animal figurines made of split willow twigs have been found tucked away in the cliffs.

By A.D. 500, a first group of Anasazi had settled in the region. They lived in dark, smoky pit-houses, hunted deer, bighorn sheep, and rabbits, and made baskets.

By A.D. 800, a second group of Anasazi began to colonize the canyon. Instead of single-family homes like those of their ancestors, they built "apartment houses" like the ones Powell found.

The Anasazi depended on seasonal rainfall for their crops. They terraced their fields and built channels and small dams to catch rain for irrigation. When the rains decreased after A.D. 1140, they were unable to grow enough food and gradually left the

Desert Culture
split-twig figure

The Anasazi built stone dams in natural drainages to hold water and soil.

region. Some scientists believe this drought lasted so long the river might have dried up altogether. By A.D. 1300, the Anasazi were gone. During the centuries that followed, the Cerbats, Hopi, Pai, Pai-ute, and Navajo Indians arrived in the canyon regions. Many of their descendants are there today.

The scenery gradually changed as the party made its way past the mouth of the San Juan

River. Instead of the usual bare rock, springs bursting out from overhanging cliffs created beautiful glens filled with oaks, ferns, and other vegetation. In the distance the men saw wonderful formations—carved walls, royal arches, alcove gulches, mounds, and monuments. They called it "Monument Canyon," but later changed the name to "Glen Canyon."

The major must have felt immense pressure to move on. By now most of their food had spoiled, and other than one mountain sheep and the occasional fish, they caught little game. The overworked and half-starved men complained to their diaries and to one another. Powell's vision of a slow and detailed exploration of the rivers and canyons had become a struggle for survival.

On August 5, the expedition entered a new canyon with limestone walls of white, gray, pink, violet, and saffron. In many places these walls were polished like glass. Below the water, waves carrying silt rubbed the stone. Above the water, rain-

STATUS REPORT
August 13, 1869
Boats and Men

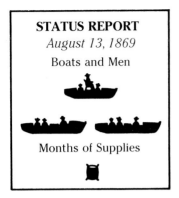

Months of Supplies

washed sand scoured the cliff face. Where the grinding current had worn into deeper layers, the Powell party found a seam of marble one thousand feet thick. They took the name "Marble Canyon" from this impressive bed of metamorphic rock.

A storm set in for several days, but the explorers moved on. The canyon walls towered higher and higher until they reached three thousand feet above the men's heads. Then in the afternoon of August 10, after seventy-one days on the river, the "Colorado Chiquito," or Little Colorado River, entered from a side canyon. This junction marked the foot of the Grand Canyon.

On August 13, the Powell party followed the river west into the Grand Canyon. Their clothes were rags, their shoes were falling apart, and only

Opposite: Marble Canyon
Photo by Gary Ladd

Grand Canyon near the mouth of the Little Colorado River
1871–72.
Photograph Archives, Utah State Historical Society

one month's worth of rations remained. Powell wrote:

> We are three quarters of a mile in the depths of the earth, and the great river shrinks into insignificance as it dashes its angry waves against the walls and cliffs that rise to the world above; they are but puny ripples, and we but pygmies, running up and down the sands, or lost among the boulders.
>
> We have an unknown distance yet to run; an unknown river yet to explore.

Virgin Mountains

Virgin River

Colorado

Separation Rapid

GRAND CANYON

River

Havasu Creek

Kanab Creek

Bright Angel Creek

Marble Canyon

Little Colorado River

MILES

0 10 20 30

5 FATES TIED TOGETHER

As Major Powell entered what was then called the "Big Canyon," he read the rock layers like the pages of a book. He said it was the "library of the gods" and gave it the name "Grand Canyon."

Its rocks began forming two billion years ago. For hundreds of millions of years the land rose and fell, hosting deserts, swamps, seas, mountains, and volcanoes. Each period left behind recognizable layers of rock. This sandwich of sediments became the Kaibab Plateau.

The Story of the Canyon Walls

The exposed walls of the Grand Canyon step back in time nearly half of the earth's geologic history.

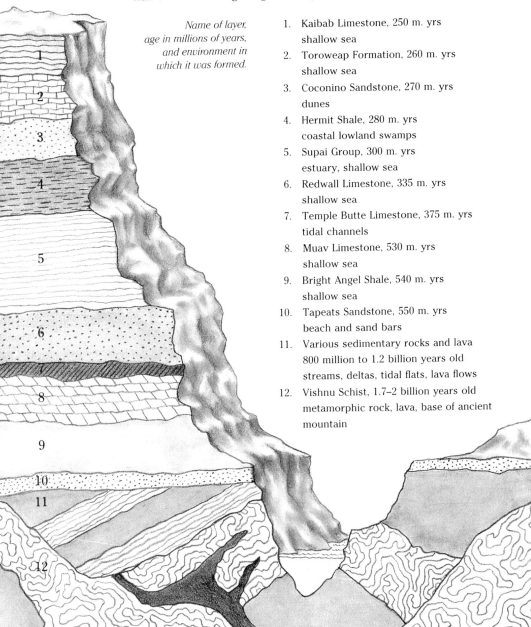

Name of layer, age in millions of years, and environment in which it was formed.

1. Kaibab Limestone, 250 m. yrs
   shallow sea
2. Toroweap Formation, 260 m. yrs
   shallow sea
3. Coconino Sandstone, 270 m. yrs
   dunes
4. Hermit Shale, 280 m. yrs
   coastal lowland swamps
5. Supai Group, 300 m. yrs
   estuary, shallow sea
6. Redwall Limestone, 335 m. yrs
   shallow sea
7. Temple Butte Limestone, 375 m. yrs
   tidal channels
8. Muav Limestone, 530 m. yrs
   shallow sea
9. Bright Angel Shale, 540 m. yrs
   shallow sea
10. Tapeats Sandstone, 550 m. yrs
    beach and sand bars
11. Various sedimentary rocks and lava
    800 million to 1.2 billion years old
    streams, deltas, tidal flats, lava flows
12. Vishnu Schist, 1.7–2 billion years old
    metamorphic rock, lava, base of ancient
    mountain

Then, about forty million years ago, the Colorado River changed direction to flow westward across this plateau. This was the beginning of the Grand Canyon. The action of the river grinding down through the ancient rock beds made the canyon deep. The eroding power of rain, ice, and wind on the canyon walls made it wide.

Not far into the Grand Canyon, the river funneled through canyon walls composed of the hardest rock the expedition had yet encountered. The major knew from experience that this meant trouble. Where the rock layers were soft and horizontal to the river, the water could flow easily through the smooth, worn channel. Where the layers were hard and dipped upstream, as in this new broken and jagged canyon, the water spilled and rolled violently.

Each day the men labored through torrential rain and blistering heat. Giant breakers bouncing off and over the boulders repeatedly capsized or swamped the boat crews. Each night they slept on rocks, unprotected from the cold and wet.

The barometers were broken, so there was no way to tell how far the river had to drop before reaching the Virgin River, their final destination.

On August 16, the men discovered a beautiful, clear stream flowing into the muddy Colorado. Powell named it "Silver Creek," although later he changed the name to "Bright Angel Creek." Up the creek's steep gorge Powell found the ruins of two or three ancient houses, a much worn milling stone, and some pottery.

The next four days, the party remained within the Grand Canyon's granite prison. With a deafening roar, the water rolled and boiled through the narrow gorge, tossing the three boats about like wood chips. Powell used extreme caution for fear any rations might be lost. Bradley wrote, "Hard

Pottery Shards

work and little distance seems to be the charac-
teristic of this canyon."

Finally, on August 21, after a wild and exciting
ten-mile ride down a winding chute, the granite
ended. Powell wrote:

> Ten miles in half a day, and limestone
> walls below. Good cheer returns;
> we forget the storms, and gloom, and
> cloud-covered canyons, and the
> black granite, and the raging river,
> and push our boats from shore in
> great glee.

For the next six days the expedition moved
quickly. They traveled past marble walls, bub-
bling springs, extinct cinder cones, and lava formations.

But on the morning of August 27, the river
switched directions to the south and began running into lower and harder formations again.

Opposite: Inner Gorge of the Grand Canyon near the junction of
the Colorado River and Bright Angel Creek
Photo by Mary Ann Fraser

Each time the river twisted to the west and away from the harder layers of rock, the men's hopes would rise. But at eleven o'clock that morning, deep within the dreaded black granite, they came upon a side stream that had washed down many large boulders. These rocks dammed the river, creating the most fearsome set of falls they had yet seen.

After studying the river below and planning a route, Powell told the men that they would be running the falls in the morning.

That night, after supper, Oramel Howland announced that he, his brother, and William Dunn had decided not to go any farther in the boats. They were sure the falls would drown them all.

Powell lay awake worrying. Should he risk the falls to finish what he came to do? Or was he leading the expedition to certain death? They had but five days of rations, yet he suspected they were close to the end of their journey. The major realized he was unwilling to leave any part of the canyon unexplored, no matter what the risk.

That morning Powell pleaded with the Howlands and Dunn to change their minds and stay with the party. But it was no use. After a breakfast "as solemn as a funeral," the three men went on their way. Each party was sure the other was taking the more dangerous route.

On August 28, 1869, Major Powell, Captain Powell, Sumner, Hall, Bradley, and Hawkins prepared to run the falls. The *Emma Dean* was so leaky it was left behind, along with Powell's fossil and mineral collections.

One after the other, they launched their boats, while the Howlands and Dunn watched from the cliffs overhead. Immediately the swift current seized them. The *Maid of the Canyon* grazed a large rock, plunged into a chute and flew over the second fall, where it was swamped by a backwashing breaker. Ahead, a great rock extended halfway across the river. Like madmen, the oarsmen pulled at the clumsy driftwood oars to control the boats, which bounded up and down through the waves at twenty miles an hour. The terrifying ride lasted only a minute, and then they were safe on shore to bail out the boats. For the major it was the greatest feat of the entire trip.

They fired their guns and waited a couple of hours, hoping their friends would rejoin the party, but they were never to see them again. Today the site is called "Separation Rapid."

After a short distance the expedition came to the head of another dangerous fall. Before Powell could stop him, Bradley stepped into the open compartment of *Kitty Clyde's Sister.*

The raging water whipped the boat back and forth, first headlong into the rocks and then back out into the stream. Bradley decided to cut the line and chance it. He had just pulled out his knife when the current ripped off the boat's stem post and set *Kitty Clyde's Sister* free.

Quickly, Bradley slid the oar into the oarlock and in one, two, three strokes turned the boat straight just as it plunged over the falls. The other five men watched Bradley vanish into the boiling white foam at the bottom of the waterfall. A moment later a dark form popped out of the waves. It was Bradley. He was standing straight up and waving his hat to signal he was all right.

Then, forgetting all caution, the major, Hawkins, and Hall leaped into *Maid of the Canyon* and away they went over the falls. Blinded by the waves rolling over them, the three men floundered until, the next thing they knew, Bradley was hauling them from the water. Sumner and Powell made the difficult climb down to join them.

Two or three more miles and they were out of the granite.

The next day, August 29, around noon, the men descended out of the Grand Canyon. As if exiting through an enormous gate, the men in two boats drifted into a large valley. Powell wrote:

> Now the danger is over. . . . The river rolls by us in silent majesty; the quiet of the camp is sweet; our joy is almost ecstasy.

The next day Powell and his men drifted to the mouth of the Virgin River. There they met four men who said that the expedition had been reported lost and that they were searching for remains.

A few miles up the Virgin River, at a Mormon

settlement, the six explorers had their first decent meal in one hundred days.

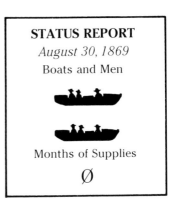

STATUS REPORT
August 30, 1869
Boats and Men

Months of Supplies
Ø

Powell gave his volunteers the two boats and all of his money. Bradley, Sumner, Hawkins, and Hall departed down the Colorado River. Bradley and Sumner later left the river at Yuma, Arizona. But in September 1869, Andy Hall and Billy Hawkins arrived at the Gulf of California. They were the first people to travel the entire length of the Colorado River.

Meanwhile the major and his brother traveled overland to St. George, Utah. Everywhere Major Powell went he asked for news of Oramel and Seneca Howland and William Dunn. Finally he learned his three friends had reached the top of the plateau. There they were killed by Shivwits Indians who had mistaken them for men who had shot a woman of their tribe.

Powell returned to Illinois and eventually to Washington as a national hero. But his first journey down the Colorado River had only strengthened his interest in the Plateau Province.

Today John Wesley Powell is known as one of the greatest western explorers, not simply because of his journeys, but because of his insight and scientific mind. He alone questioned the pattern of settlement and development in the west.

In 1873, Powell became commissioner of Indian Affairs. His work led to the founding of the Smithsonian Institution's Bureau of Ethnology. He visited the western tribes to collect information about the Indians—stories, languages, and genealogy. He had photographs taken to record their images for the future. Unfortunately, when he made photos to be sold to the public and not for science, he sometimes dressed the Indians to fit easterners' ideas of how Indians "ought" to look.

Though Powell wanted the Indians to preserve their traditions and languages, he also encouraged them to learn English and become more like other Americans. Where the Indians' conditions were very bad, he told them to leave their homes and move to a reservation. He believed these changes were their only hope of escaping the

Major Powell talking to a member of the Paiutes living on the Kaibab Plateau near the Grand Canyon
Photograph Archives, Utah State Historical Society

poverty and disease that threatened them. Today many Native Americans value their own traditions and resent having been forced to adopt outsiders' ways.

Powell was one of the first people to predict the strain settlement and development would place on the West's limited resources. By 1888, his foresight had won him the position of director of the Irrigation Survey. As the nation's most powerful geographer, he was responsible for determining which land parcels were fit for settlement. He knew land had little value without water. He proposed a cooperative system of water management. This was an idea that he had borrowed from the Mormons of Utah, who had learned how to survive in the desert. But Powell's plan was blocked by wealthy landowners and companies that already controlled the best streams. It was not until 1902, when President Theodore Roosevelt asked Congress to create a federal irrigation program, that Powell's ideas were appreciated.

Opposite: Lake Powell at dusk
Photo by Gary Ladd

Major Powell once predicted, "All the waters of all the arid lands will eventually be taken from their natural channels." He was right. In 1963, a dam was built that flooded beautiful Glen Canyon. It formed the longest artificial lake in the United States, Lake Powell. Today the West's increasing demand for water has made the Colorado River System one of the most controlled in the world. It has been nearly regulated out of existence by reservoirs, dams, pumping stations, hydroelectric plants, and hundreds of miles of aqueducts, canals, and tunnels. Now, the Colorado River often runs out of water before it reaches the Gulf of California.

From the time of the ancient Anasazi cliff dwellers to the present, water has been the key to life in the Colorado River region. As Powell predicted, how we manage our limited resources in the face of increased demand will decide who can live there, and for how long. And, as Powell showed, only by appreciating the beauty and power of the earth can we learn to live well on it.

BIBLIOGRAPHY

Ayer, Eleanor H. *The Anasazi.* New York: Walker & Company, 1993.

Buff, Mary and Conrad. *The Colorado: River of Mystery.* Los Angeles: Ward Ritchie Press, 1968.

Carlson, Vada F. *John Wesley Powell, Conquest of the Canyon.* Irvington-on-Hudson, NY: Harvey House, 1974.

Carrier, Jim. "The Colorado: A River Drained Dry." *National Geographic* (June 1991):4–35.

Foster, Lynne. *Exploring the Grand Canyon: Adventures of Yesterday & Today.* Grand Canyon: Grand Canyon Natural History Association, 1990.

Fowler, Don D., Robert C. Euler, and Catherine S. Fowler, *John Wesley Powell and the Anthropology of the Canyon Country.* Washington, D.C.: United States Government Printing Office, 1969.

Gaines, Ann. *John Wesley Powell and the Great Surveys of the American West.* New York: Chelsea House, 1991.

Jones, Jayne C. *The American Indian in America,* vol. 2, *Early 19th Century to the Present.* Minneapolis: Lerner Publications Company, 1970.

Krutch, Joseph W. *Grand Canyon: Today and All Its Yesterdays.* New York: William Sloane Associates, 1958.

Lavender, David. *Colorado River Country.* New York: E.P. Dutton, Inc., 1982.

Miller, Peter. "John Wesley Powell: Vision for the West." *National Geographic* (April 1994):86–115.

Powell, John Wesley. *The Exploration of the Colorado River and Its Canyons.* New York: Dover Publications, 1961.

Stegner, Wallace. *Beyond the Hundredth Meridian.* Boston: Houghton Mifflin Co., 1954.

Stevens, Larry. *The Colorado River in Grand Canyon.* Flagstaff, AZ: Red Lake Books, 1983.

Tamarin, Alfred and Shirley Glubok. *Ancient Indians of the Southwest.* Garden City, NY: Doubleday & Co., Inc., 1975.

Utah State Historical Society. *Utah Historical Quarterly,* vol. xv. Salt Lake City: Utah State Historical Society, 1947.

Wallace, Robert. *The Grand Canyon—The American Wilderness.* Chicago: Time Life Books, 1972.

INDEX

Anasazi, 40–42, *42*
Antecedent rivers, theory of,
    11
Army, U.S., 29
Ashley, William, 13–14, 22
Ashley Falls, 11–14

Barometers, *17*, 22, 51
Bradley, George, 8, 23, 24, 26,
    32, 36, 38, 51–53, 55, 57,
    58, 59
Bright Angel Creek, 51
Bureau of Ethnology, 60

Cataract Canyon, 38–39
"Cataract of Lodore, The"
    (Southey), 18–19
Cerbats, 42
Chicago Tribune, 17–18
Colorado Plateau, 11, 60
Colorado River, 3–4, *5*, 5–6, 64
    change in course of, 50

joining of Green River and,
    35, 35–36
Powell party's exploration
    of, 3, 37–59
Compasses, *17*
Congress, U.S., 62

Desert Culture, 41, *41*
Desolation Canyon, *31*, 31–32
Dirty Devil Creek, 39–40
Disaster Falls, 22
Dunn, Bill, 7, 22, 39, 54, 55, 59

Emma Dean, 8, 9, *9*, 19, 20, 32,
    39, 55

Flaming Gorge, 9–11, *10*
Fossils, 10–11, 55

Glen Canyon, 43, 64
Goodman, Frank, 8, 19–21, 28,
    30, 32

68

Sextants, *17*
Shivwits Indians, 59
Smithsonian Institution, 60
Southey, Robert, 18–19
Sumner, Jack, 7, 20–21, 22, 55, 58, 59

Thermometers, *17*
Transcontinental railroad, 4, 15–16, 34
Tsau-wi-at, 30

Uinta Indians, 28
Uinta River, 26, 28, 30
Utes, 30

Virgin River, 51, 58–59

Whirlpool Canyon, 26

Yampa River, 25